Women of Faith
Living the Dream

Accepting the Call to Leadership-
Leading Where You Are

Jocelyn Whitfield

PRESS

Table of Contents

Dedication and Acknowledgements

*T*his book is dedicated to my spiritual daughters, mentees, sister friends, nieces, cousins, siblings and every woman who struggles with the call to leadership.

May every page bring you closer to God's purpose for your life and empower you to accept your assignment to lead wherever you are.

I would also like to thank the many Christian women who have been models of excellence in leadership and to whom I honor as my mentors.

I want to specially acknowledge my friend and colleague who helped edit this book, June Mickens. June you are the angel God sent my way. To my son, Aaron, thank you for honouring and supporting the call of leadership upon my life.

Forward

I n a most delightful and challenging scripture on women's high privilege and profound call to prosper and make a significant difference in the world in which they live, this inspiring biblical observation is made on a women of God; ''She speaks with wisdom and faithful instruction is on her tongue.' This is how I felt as I read Jocelyn's book, <u>Women of Faith</u>. I have personally been acquainted with Jocelyn Whitfield for many ears. Upon each encounter with her, regardless of the season of life she was in, I was inspired by her love for God, and her deep commitment to see other women grow in their faith in the Lord, as well as fulfill and run with God's dream for their lives.

That's what this book is about – Living and fulfilling God's creative dreams, purposes and plans for your life as a woman of faith. Jocelyn shares from her own rich experience of serving and working in her home, church, work place, and community. When she encourages women to pray about their productive involvement in the marketplace, in politics, and in their local communities, she breathes a breath of fresh air into the unlimited possibilities women have to change their world by utilizing their dreams, gifts, and talents to powerfully serve others.

This book itself is a significant fulfillment to one of Jocelyn's personal dreams. And even as she fulfilled one of her important dreams, she stands as a mentor, teacher and a coach enthusiastically cheering on other women to become "Women of Faith; Living the Dream and Answering the Call."

Good job, Jocelyn! May many, many, women be set free to dream their own God-given dreams as they read and ponder the content of this inspiring book.

> Dotty Schmitt, Pastor,
> Author, Teacher
> Immanuel's Church, Silver Spring, MD

Preface

T oday God is calling women to lead in extraordinary ways. Women of faith are becoming God's instruments, evangelists and sentinels in the marketplace, community and the world. As women of faith we have been called to leadership for the purpose of making a difference in this world, and fulfilling the dreams that God has placed in our hearts.... *wherever we are or He assigns us.*

If you have dreams of becoming a leader or aspiring to be one, it is my hope that within the pages of this book you will discover new dreams or recover your old ones, discern God's heart for you, examine the variety of ways that you can lead, and utilize some of the essential resources that God has provided to make your dreams a reality.

I believe that regardless of your age and season of life, it is never too late to live your dreams. I am sure you have a few. *The good news is no matter when your dreams were conceptualized, every day is a new opportunity for your dreams to come true if you place your trust and faith in God.*

Chapter 1

Women of Faith: Living the Dream and Answering the Call

"Some men see things as they are and say 'why?' I dream of things that never were and say 'why not?'" ~George Bernard Shaw

D o you sense that there is more to life than you are living? Are there dreams that you have hidden in your heart that have not been realized? You may feel that it is too late and you are too old or that you lack professional credentials. Whatever your reason, it may appear that your dreams may never come true. But, with God, all things are possible to those who believe.

Can you believe that He has a dream in mine that only you can fulfill? Yes, no matter what your station in life, God is calling you to partner with Him and join His leadership team. Becoming a leader and partnering with God has little to do with gender, your status in the church or in the market-place, authority, prestige, occupation, power, privilege, rank, hierarchy, knowledge, or skills. All of those things are a part of the world's view. God calls us to partnership with Him for the purpose of accomplishing His will in the earth.

For we have not only been saved, but called with a holy calling, not according to our works, but according to God's purpose and grace (2 Timothy 1:9). In Christ, we have been given a holy invitation to be instruments of His grace and to be used as His agents as He changes the hearts of men for eternity.

You may feel disqualified by your past. The good news is that God calls us despite our yesterdays. As we examine scripture, we discover that God has called some of the most unlikely people to partnership and leadership. What about Moses, the murderer, and David, the adulterer? What about Paul, the chief persecutor of Christians? What about Rehab, the harlot, and the pregnant and unmarried Mary, the mother of Jesus?

God is calling us as well. I know that, when I was called to serve women, I didn't think I was the right person for the job. After all, to be perfectly honest with you, I have never had a great fondness for women or desired to be around them for too long. (Awful, I know!) Besides the lack of desire, I didn't feel equipped to serve them in any capacity. You see, to that point, most my experiences and relationships with women had been quite poor. Except for my sisters, cousins, and few female friends, I found my relationships with women often to be contentious, condescending, and hurtful. There was pettiness, cliques, gossip, and jealousy that always seemed to surface when women came together. And, I wanted none of it!

So, if these were my feelings, why would I spend the last 20 years motivating, inspiring, mentoring, and developing women spiritually and personally? It's simple. I said "yes" to God when He called and assigned me to this work with women. I said, "Yes" to the very thing that was unthinkable, unnatural, least satisfying, and incongruent with my life's choice, all because *He* called me. Since then, I've worked tirelessly with women. God has a way of turning our dislikes and the things we abhor into His purposes and callings.

All of us have been called. Some of us have been called to plant seeds and others to water with His Words. We all have specific ways in which we can contribute to the cause of Christ. The question is whether we say "yes" to our Lord when He calls. You may feel that you are not equipped. Guess what? He calls the unequipped so that we don't feel that we're functioning on our own. After all, God is really the only One who can equip us. God has a dream and desire that only you can help Him realize. There is only one acceptable response to this call to lead and that is to say "Yes, Lord, I will."

Answering the call does not automatically translate into a special position or seat of power; however, this may happen in some cases. Instead, answering the call means that we are afforded the grand opportunity to partner with God and to serve Him with everything that we have. Being called to ministry is a noble honor. Just think: God is calling you to serve Him. Ministry is serving, and serving is ministry.

Every one of us, who is in Christ, has been called to ministry. Now, this statement may be uncomfortable for you because the words *ministry* or *minister* have been somewhat misused in the Christian community and perceived by many to be something other than serving. We tend to view *minister* as a particular position held in church or within a congregation, and by doing so, we often establish a superficial spiritual hierarchy within the church. However, this is contrary to what Jesus taught and modelled. He made himself of no reputation but took on the form of a servant, and was made in to the likeness of men (Philippians 2:7). He came not to be ministered unto, but to minister, and to give His life a ransom for many (Matt 20:28). Jesus has made it plain that any disciple who wants to achieve greatness in God's kingdom has to take on the role of servant. Jesus said that, if you want to be the greatest in the Kingdom, to influence and lead others, you have to become a servant first (Matthew 23:2-12).

Therefore, we, who are the called of the Lord, are ministers. We are called to serve...to become His feet, His hands, and His voice. We are called to encourage the oppressed, share our human resources, heal the sick and broken hearted, spread the love and compassion of Christ, and influence others to follow Him. We have been called to be servant leaders wherever God calls us to serve.

It is my hope and desire that, as a woman of faith, you will say, as Erma Bombeck once said, *"When I stand before God, ... I would not have a single bit of talent left and could say I've used everything that you gave me."*

Questions for Personal Reflection

What have you been called to do? Read Ephesians 4:1 – 3.

How are you serving as the feet, hands, and voice of Jesus?

Chapter 2

God's Special Treasure

"And the Lord declared this day that you are His people, His special treasure, as He promised." Deuteronomy 26:18 (NLT)

L adies, we are God's special treasure. We are a royal diadem, a crown of splendor in the hands of the Lord (Isaiah 62:3). We are His extraordinary jewels, His diamonds and rubies to be worn as an expression of His love and grace. We are not forsaken or forgotten. He has great utility for our lives. We are so very loved by Him that He gave us Christ to liberate us and to give us identity and purpose.

While Jesus was on the earth, He challenged and transcended the customs and double standards men held concerning women. He redefined the woman's role, defying customs of that day and breaking down the walls that divided men from women.

Let's take a look at Jesus' relationships with a few women.

There was a woman who was caught in adultery, and the men of that day wanted to stone her to death because of the Law of Moses. (Interestingly, they brought the woman to

Jesus but neglected to bring the man also involved in the forbidden act.) Yet, Jesus rebuked them and exposed their sin. And, instead of condemning the woman, Jesus encouraged her to go and leave her life of sin (John 8:3 – 11).

Jesus also spoke to women publically and privately. In John 4:4 – 23, we see Jesus engaged in a conversation not just with a woman, but with a Samaritan woman who had been married five times and was then living with a man who was not her husband. It was not only unacceptable to be seen with a woman with such a background, but it was disdainful for a Jew to engage or be seen with a Samaritan. Nonetheless, here was Jesus interacting with this Samaritan woman – a surprise to her and to the disciples. However, this very act changed a woman, and a city, because she returned home to tell others about Christ. She became an influencer and a leader, preaching about a Christ who knew all about her and yet accepted her. As a result of her transformation and testimony, others were encouraged to seek Christ.

Scripture tells us of other women, such as Mary Magdalene, who became Jesus' companions and followers. Mary Magdalene was possessed by many demons until Jesus delivered her. After her deliverance, she became Christ's disciple and friend. She was the first person to whom He appeared after the resurrection (Mark 16:9 – 10), and she was the initial carrier of the resurrection message. Clearly, Jesus could have chosen anyone for such a critical role, but He chose a woman to carry the gospel – the good news of His resurrection from the dead.

There were other women among Jesus' disciples and friends. Mary and Martha, the sisters of Lazarus, were disciples, friends, and companions of Christ. He often visited them in their home and enjoyed their company, fellowship, and hospitality. While in their home, He allowed Mary to sit at His feet as He taught the men about the wonders of God, even though the Law of Moses forbade women to be taught the Torah (Luke 10:38 – 42). We also know that they and Lazarus were close to the Savior's heart, as He wept with them, comforted them, worked a miracle in their presence, and allowed them to anoint Him in preparation for burial. (John 11:17 – 44; 12:1 – 8).

Jesus' treatment of women influenced others. Luke writes about Anna, the prophetess and daughter of Phanuel, who served God with fasting and prayer night and day (Luke 2:36-37). The Apostle Paul appreciated the gifting of women and partnered with many to establish the early church and sustain it in his absence. Among them were Lydia, an entrepreneur who sold purple and linen in the marketplace and used her house as a refuge for the apostles (Acts 16:14, 15), and Phoebe, the deaconess (Romans 16:1, 2). There also was

Priscilla, wife of Aquila, who lived, worked, and travelled with the Apostle Paul (Acts 18; Romans 16:3 – 5).

Through Jesus, Luke, Paul, and others, God makes it clear that women are essential partners in proclaiming the gospel and in equipping the church of Jesus Christ, just as our brothers are. Christ has affirmed us and still affirms us. We are living in the day foreseen by the Prophet Joel (Joel 3:28, 29). God's Spirit has been poured out on all flesh and, as His sons and daughters, we have been called to prophesy, preach the gospel, and proclaim the counsel of the Lord. We have been called to join our brothers and sisters in the greatest commission of all – to become partners in proclaiming Christ for the salvation of souls.

The church must be very careful in this hour in its treatment of women. *If we choose to suppress the voice of women, we could be suppressing and rejecting the voice of God.* We could be rejecting the voice that He has chosen in this season to speak through, to touch, and to play a part in transforming lives for His kingdom.

Women and men alike have been called to be Christ followers – His disciples – and to disciple others (Mark 16:15). Isn't it great that we have not been forgotten and no longer are in bondage?

We can thank our Lord that, through Him, we have been given a new life and, through this new life, we can enjoy the freedom and liberation that He has given us. Women who were subject to dishonor, abuse, persecution, and inferiority are now loosed, set free, and restored to right relationship with God. In this liberation, we find freedom to do and preach the gospel anytime, anyplace, and anywhere! This liberation began before the early church with Christ and continues today with women being recognized as leaders around the world.

Gender barriers are being broken. Some make their mark as pastors, evangelists, teachers, and bishops in churches and assemblies. However, we also see God's daughters actively impacting the world for Christ through a range of other roles. In politics, we see women vying for, and achieving, some of the highest positions in our world. Others are among the top corporate executives and in place on the highest courts in the land. As mothers, wives, and singles, we are expanding our territory and extending our sphere of influence. Wherever we are, we are embarking on uncharted waters, with God as our captain, to fulfil our purpose in God's redemptive plan for mankind.

Ladies, we have a grand future. We can anticipate an awesome partnership with our God as He uses our gifting, talents, knowledge, abilities, and skills for His purposes and plans.

Questions for Personal Reflection

How has God liberated you, and from what has He liberated you?

What are the talents and gifts that He has given you?

How will you use these gifts for His purposes?

Chapter 3

Your Dream Isn't Big Enough

"We grow great by dreams. All big men are dreamers. Woodrow Wilson, 28th President of the U.S.

C an you believe that God's dreams for you are bigger than any you may have for yourself? His dreams and possibilities wait to be realized by you. If you haven't done any dreaming yet, begin today. Everyone should have a personal dream or vision for their lives.

When we dream, we envision our potential and life's possibilities. A dream is like a flame put to dry wood; it ignites passion, which can translate into action and become the engine that propels your life in a certain direction. Dreams aren't just what our minds engage in while we sleep. Some dreams come from God. We see in the Bible that God spoke to His prophets through dreams and visions in days past. He is still speaks to us today in visions and dreams. Yes, the very dreams that are in your heart have been planted by God. You may think that these pursuits and aspirations have come about on your own accord but I believe that God has a dream in mind for each of us personally and spiritually. God has a unique plan for your life and he will help you achieve it.

Whatever your dreams, you have a God who says that it is never too late. For with him all things are possible. It's never too late to dream. As we surrender to his dreams for us, we find peace, tranquillity, purpose, fulfilment and success.

We all know people who dream and dream, and their dreams never amount to anything. So, how do we know that our dreams are more than passing fancies? One clue that a dream may be something more is that it is unfathomable and unrelenting. That is, it continues to bob up no matter how many different activities you become involved in or no matter the season of your life. Even in the midst of dimness and doubt, it continues to burn somewhere deep within – a constant reminder of an idea, a desire, or a plan that is still waiting to be birthed.

When we dream, we are in the company of great people who have been given dreams by God. Think about Joseph, who was called "a dreamer." He was given a dream that he would rule over his brothers and they would bow down to him. Sharing this dream with his brothers infuriated them and, though they didn't kill him as they'd planned, it landed him in Egypt and a slave in the house of Potiphar, who was Pharoah's captain of the guard. However, dreams continued to play a pivotal role in Joseph's life. While in prison following his refusal to give in to the advances of Potiphar's wife, God allowed him to interpret the dreams of two fellow prisoners – Pharoah's baker and cupbearer. Later, when Pharoah could find nobody to interpret his dream, the cupbearer remembered and recommended Joseph. Not only did God permit Joseph again to interpret a dream, but He gave Joseph wisdom to devise a solid action plan for Pharoah in dealing with the situation forecasted in the dream. Little did Joseph know that Pharoah would find favor with him and assign him the chief role in carrying out the action plan? Little did he know that his own family would be impacted by the famine, travel to Egypt for provisions, and (as dreamed years before and although unknowingly) submit to little brother Joseph. And, little did Joseph know that, in the end, God would use him to honor His covenant with Abraham to sustain his seed for the generations to follow. The dream that God gave Joseph became a reality, but it was not immediate and not without challenges and obstacles.

I am sure that fear and doubt entered Joseph's mind and heart from time to time, as it does with us. However, he continued in faith and persevered through every challenge and obstacle, believing in his God. And, we can too.

Just know that challenges and obstacles are a part of the process. Every dream will be tested. This too is a part of the process. The process is good for us, even though we may feel badly at times. The process serves as a filter or refiner of those things that will ultimately interfere with bringing our dreams to fruition. The refinery process will weed out inflated egos, pride, selfish motives, and other impurities and replace them with patience and perseverance. We discover in the process that our dreams can only be achieved through the work of the Spirit in our lives and our reliance on the author and finisher of our faith, for it is He who has begun this work and will bring it to completion, so that our dreams coincide with His kingdom purposes. God's dreams for our lives are always bigger than anything we can think or imagine. Scriptures tells us that God's thoughts and ways are higher than ours (Isaiah 55:9).

This book that you are reading is a dream come true. Even though years have passed since the concept was placed on my heart, the thought of writing this book never left me. The concept would bob up when least expected. In the midst of my work responsibilities, caring for others, or even working in the ministry, the idea of this book would find a way back in my heart and mind. Then, once I finally began writing the book, obstacles would creep in, stealing time, health, and energy and making demands on my quiet time. These were the times that I had to rely on God's promises; reminders of His faithfulness from the past, often found through entries in my journals, and my undying belief that all things are possible with God.

Over the years, I have found journaling a valuable tool to keep my dreams constantly before me. I have recorded my dreams, aspirations, challenges, successes, feelings, desires, the words that God has spoken to me through scripture and sometimes the dates that prayers have been answered. In times when my faith wanes and doubts surface, the words recorded, and the answers to prayer, become a source of inspiration as reminders of God's faithfulness.

So, how do you move toward achieving your dreams?

Write out your dreams. Revisit them often so you will not forget them. Spend time with God, and be still and quiet, listening carefully for His voice and direction; God will reveal the next steps that you should take.

Choose to trust God's faithfulness, and think of the times in your life when God has answered your prayers. Again, here is where journaling pays off. The pages of your journal often will document the proof of answered prayers, and these remind you of God's faithfulness.

Be mindful that our expectation and hope rest in the God for whom nothing is impossible – a fact that can keep you motivated when everything seems to be going wrong. Remember that God is the creator of all earth and the chief financier of the universe. Do not lose heart or faint; God has the power to change your situation. He is just waiting to enable you to move past it or to be an overcomer through it.

Become like a bull dog; hold on to your dream with all the tenacity of your faith.

Honestly, you are the only one who can kill your dreams. No one else can.

We kill our dreams with our mouths, thoughts, actions, or non-actions. With our lips, we can speak life to our dreams. And, sometimes, we also speak death, lack, and inadequacy. Our tongues can be deadly members and can wreak havoc in our lives (James 3), if we do not learn to control them. We can curse or bless; that is our choice. But, the words of every believer should be life–producing; that's because the life giver resides in us. Look back at the creation story. Everything that has been created was spoken into existence by the words of God (Genesis 1). You can keep your dreams alive by the words that come from your mouth, because life and death are in the power our tongues (Proverbs 18:21).

Keeping our thoughts in check is equally important to our dreams. What a man thinks is what he is (Proverbs 23:7). Our thoughts should be harmonious with what God's word says. When we allow our thoughts to be negative, they can paralyze us, preventing our dreams from becoming a reality.

There is another factor related to our thought process. Often, what we think about is what we act on. A battle constantly goes on in our minds. This battle is between negative and good thoughts. In order for the good to prevail, we have to be conscious of our thoughts and bring every thought into captivity to the obedience of Christ (2 Corinthians 10:5).

Only through renewing our minds with the word of God can our thoughts be transformed and controlled. Feeding on God's word is the only thing that can counteract our thoughts. We literally have to cast down every thought that goes against the truth according to God's word. Then, we must begin declaring God's words over every negative thought until our thoughts line up with God's words.

For instance, let's say that you have a dream of opening up a child care center. However, every thought seems to suggest that this is an impossibility because you do not have the necessary finances to achieve this.

How do you move forward? Every time you think about your dream, and certainly every time you're plagued with those funding concerns, remind yourself (aloud if necessary) that *your* God shall supply all *your* needs and that no good thing will God withhold from you (including the things to make dreams, aligned with His word, come true). As you speak words like these, you will begin to think the way God thinks.

Make a point to meditate on things consistent with God's word. As believers, we are to think on things that are true, noble, reputable, authentic, compelling, gracious – the best, not the worst; the beautiful, not the ugly; things to praise, not things to curse. When we put into practice these things, God will make everything work together for our good (Philippians 4:7-8).

Lastly, be expectant. Anticipate and prepare for the birth of your dream. Be like a pregnant woman as she waits for the arrival of her child. Everything she does is done with expectancy and to ensure the health and viability of that child yet to be born.

So it is with our dreams. We should have the same type of expectancy. We should be preparing and taking action, moving towards its delivery. Just remember. God is able to do exceedingly abundantly above anything that we can ask or think, beyond our wildest dreams, according to His power in us. It is His pleasure to give us all things pertaining life and godliness.

So reach back, and revisit your dreams. Present them to the Lord, and wait on His direction regarding them. If the response is that you should move forward, open your mouth and declare what you are dreaming. Meditate on scriptures that affirm your dreams. Be expectant, and have faith in God's ability to bring what He has put in your heart to pass.

Remember, it is never too late; and you are never too old to renew and reinvigorate your God-given dreams. He is the God in which nothing is impossible if we believe.

Questions for Personal Reflection

Read Genesis 37:5 – 8.

Did Joseph have a dream? What were some of his challenges, and how did he handle them?

Do you have a dream that has not become a reality?

What are some of the challenges that you have faced in achieving your dreams?

Chapter 4

You Can Conquer Fear

"Do not fear, little flock, for it is your Father's good pleasure to give you the kingdom." Luke 12:32

F ear can be our enemy or the best thing we possess. First, there is the fear of God, which involves our reverence and respect for our Creator, the Almighty, who is over us all. Such fear extols His greatness and who He is, just because He is. In this type of reverential fear, we acknowledge that there is no one or nothing equal or comparable to, nor as excellent, powerful, or good as God.

Then there is the second type of fear, and this fear has very little to do with God. It is the fear that rules and takes captive our senses, emotions, and actions; it is fear that devastates our dreams and aspirations. Such fear comes straight from Satan, who throughout creation has used such fear as a weapon against us to defeat us –.literally paralyzing our actions and impeding our dreams. Fear of this nature has the capacity to rob us of our peace in the present and the future. It is the cause of worry, anxiety, tension, stress, and failure. It causes us to see lack instead of plenty, failure instead of victory, as well as death and dread instead of life and fulfilment.

You can be sure that God is not the author of that second type of fear. We have not been called to be fearful, but rather to be strong and courageous. Scripture reminds us that we need not fear, because God promises never to fail us, leave us, or forsake us (Deuteronomy 31:6; Isaiah 41:10). We don't have to be uncertain about this. He is the light of our salvation, so in whom shall we fear or dread? He is our refuge and stronghold, so in whom should we be afraid? (Psalm 27:1) He has not given us the spirit of fear, timidity, or cowardice, but He given us love, power, a calm and well-balanced mind, discipline, and self-controlled spirit (2 Timothy 1:7).

If we do not conquer fear, it is doubtful that we will fulfil the dreams that we have for ourselves, much less reach the destiny that God has planned for us. The Bible has a lot to say about fear and faith.

In Matthew, we read about Jesus withering the leaves of the fig tree. When asked about it by the disciples, Jesus responded to them, and shares with us today that, if we have faith (a firm relying trust) and do not doubt, we can not only do what was done to the fig tree, but even tell a mountain to be moved, and it will be done (Matthew 21:18 – 21).

In the book of James, we are told that, when we bring our requests to God, we are to come in faith without wavering (translation: no hesitating or doubting). Because, if we waiver, we will not receive anything of the Lord (James 1:6 – 7). Trusting God, that is activating our faith and watching Him work time-and-time again, is one way to combat fear.

Think back with me to the story of two women who lost much – Ruth and Naomi. (See the Book of Ruth.) Early on, we see, Naomi responding in a very bitter way to the loss of her husband, sons, extended family, and security. Yet, though bitter initially, I believe she still had faith in her God. Nonetheless, while still lamenting over her circumstances, she decided to return to her extended family in Bethlehem.

Enter woman #2 – Ruth. Ruth was one of Naomi's daughters-in-law and, following Naomi's decision to go back home, Ruth was encouraged (as was her sister-in-law Orpah) to return to her own family. However, Ruth had come to love her mother-in-law and, in one of the most impassioned portions of scripture, pledged her loyalty to Naomi.

Though she loved Naomi, I am sure that Ruth had to have been at least somewhat apprehensive about what would be a completely new life for her in Bethlehem. Just think of all of the unknowns – moving from the comfort of your family and your culture, and needing to embrace a new God, a new people, a new region, and a new way of life. She probably feared that she would be rejected because she was a Moabite. I imagine there also were doubts about her future should something happen to Naomi. All of that had to have been frightening! Yet, I believe there must have been something about the way Naomi reverenced her God that attracted Ruth and gave her the sense that following Naomi was the right decision.

Fast forward to the women's arrival in Bethlehem. It was harvest time. Naomi learned that a relative of her husband, named Boaz, owned a grain field, and she thought that they could glean in his field – that is, pick up the leftovers of Boaz' team. Instead of seeing her mother-in-law go out and do such hard work, Ruth offered. While in the field, she caught the attention of Boaz, found favor in his sight, and later became his wife.

This story is more than one of courage, friendship, love, and mentorship. It is also a story of faith vs. fear. Ruth didn't let what she saw with her own eyes (lack), and what she heard (bitterness), keep her from moving forward toward a dream of a better life. She took a risk, moved in faith, and trusted in the One whom initially was only Naomi's God. In doing so, though, she gained favor with God and, through His divine will, favor with Boaz as well. What Naomi and Ruth didn't know was that God had already made provision for them, even before they journeyed to Bethlehem. And, that provision was activated by Ruth's willingness to move beyond her fear and step out (in her case literally) in faith. In the end, she not only received provision but protection, spiritual insight, love, and fulfilled dreams.

You and I are no different than Naomi and Ruth. We've all faced fear at one time or another. The potential for fear is always present and can take hold of anyone. However, we don't have to let it take hold of us.

Take Peter for example, probably the best-known of Christ's disciples. Peter was in a boat with the other disciples and saw someone walking toward them…on the water. He, and his fellow disciples, became frightened. (And, who wouldn't?) So, to calm their fears, Jesus identified himself, but Peter wasn't entirely convinced and asked Jesus to confirm his identity by allowing him to walk on the water too. Well, Jesus beckoned Peter to come, and you've got to give it to Peter, he not only got out of the boat, but he also began walking on the water. The problem was that Peter's stroll was short-lived. He started looking around him, at the winds and the waves, and he became fearful. He began to rely on his senses – what he felt and saw – and he lost his focus on Jesus, who had given him the power to do something phenomenal and was out there in the water with him, encouraging him to come. But, here's the good thing. When Peter felt himself in trouble, he did the right thing – he cried out to Jesus. Immediately, Jesus reached out His hand, caught Peter, and drew him back to the safety of the boat (Matthew 14:20-31). Peter was on the path to something great, but he let fear trip him up.

When we look at our circumstances or at the opposition that could keep us from achieving our dreams, fear is likely to raise its head. However, when that happens, you have a choice – let fear take you captive, or rebuke it and trust God and his faithfulness to show you the way. I hope you know that you can trust God. He'll always be there (Matthew 28:20). So, if God is always with us, then we have the power to overcome fear.

To walk in faith, or in fear, is a choice. Our faith comes from God, but God develops that faith in us through our experiences with Him. If we are open to Him, He allows us to become closer and closer to Him through every experience, and it's in those experiences that we learn to trust God more and see that we actually have no reason to fear. Experience with God provides opportunities to see just how He has been faithful to us throughout our lives and, because of His faithfulness in the past, to trust Him both with our current and future challenges and dreams.

The answer to fear is God's faithfulness toward us, His love for us, and His power in us. However, to reap the benefits of that answer, we have to make a firm decision to trust God. We must exercise the faith that He has given us and stay focused on His ability to bring our dreams to pass. This may not seem logical, but it is biblical, and so many of us can tell you from personal experience that it is real as well.

There is a choice that every God-inspired dreamer must make? Will I trust in God, who has planted the seed of dreams in me and who has the power and the desire to make those dreams come true? Will I allow fear and doubt to rob me of my present and future destiny? That's the choice. How will you choose?

Questions for Personal Reflection

Why is fear the greatest killer of dreams?

Does fear come from God? (Read 2 Timothy 1:7, James 1:5 – 8, and Psalm 27:1.)

Can fear be a destroyer of faith? How?

Why shouldn't we fear?

Chapter 5

Empowered by the Holy Spirit

"I'm telling you these things while I'm still living with you. The Friend, the Holy Spirit whom the Father will send at my request, will make everything plain to you. He will remind you of all the things I have told you. I'm leaving you well and whole. That's my parting gift to you. Peace. I don't leave you the way you're used to being left—feeling abandoned, bereft. So don't be upset. Don't be distraught." John 14:25-27 (Message Bible)

A chieving our dreams not only takes faith in God and confronting our fears, but it also requires being empowered by the Holy Spirit. When we choose to tap into the power of the indwelling Spirit, there are no limits to what we can accomplish.

As women, we are in an unprecedented moment of time. We have a mandate from God to lead and influence in extraordinary ways. In each of us, there is a reservoir of unrelenting and supernatural power that is ours because of Christ, and that power is the Holy Spirit.

Jesus viewed this empowerment of the Holy Spirit as essential to doing the work that we have been called to do. At His departure, Christ asked the Father to give us another comforter, who would be in us to counsel, help, guide, advocate, enable, and stand by us (John 14:16). We have been given a personal GPS in the person of the Holy Spirit, to configure the pathway to our destination and navigate us to the fulfilment of our dreams. He is equipped to do this because He is full of wisdom from the Father. All we need to do is to follow His direction.

As we think about the Holy Spirit in our lives, we see a number of roles. He is the giver of spiritual gifts that are critical if we are to lead effectively. For instance, we have been given the gift of wisdom to help us live well and judiciously, the gift of knowledge to see into the deeper underlying purposes of God, and the gift of discernment to enable us to distinguish between truth and falsehood (1 Corinthians 12:1 – 14).

Enablement gifts also are given to us by the Holy Spirit. Those include the gift of administration, encouragement, giving, healing, and teaching, among others (Romans 12:6 – 8).

Every believer has been given such gifts according to God's design and grace, and they are intended for our good and the good of others. So, when God gives us a job to do, He also equips us so that we do not have to rely on our own natural abilities alone.

I have been privileged to serve in many capacities professionally, in the local church, and in the community. And, I can tell you that the positions I've held have had very little to do with extraordinary brilliance or academic degrees. Rather, they rest solely on my reliance upon the Holy Spirit and the favor of God. It is through His guidance, direction, and supernatural ability that doors were opened and opportunities were afforded me. The indwelling Spirit of God has been my guide, friend, and enabler.

It's important to know that the Holy Spirit is always speaking to us to show us how to respond to the situations of life. He speaks to us through scripture, inner promptings, and wise counsel. There have been times in my life when the Holy Spirit has spoken to me through a movie, while watching TV, reading a book, searching the Internet, or driving my car. Through these avenues, He has illuminated certain words or concepts, or has sent a revelation.

Because I never know when the Spirit will share something with me, I've made it a practice to have a notebook or recorder handy at all times. Keeping something at hand to record what you receive in your spirit, as direction from the Holy Spirit, is critical. If you don't record it, it's likely that you will not be able to remember the direction given. Remember, the Holy Spirit can speak to you anywhere, and His empowerment gives us what we need to succeed.

As women of faith, a great opportunity awaits us as we are called to lead. We can embrace the wonderful gift of the Holy Spirit, granted by our heavenly Father, and understand that there is nothing we cannot do because of Him (Jeremiah 32:17). All we need to is to "ask and it will be given to us; seek and we will find; knock and the door will be opened to us. For everyone who asks receives, and he who seeks finds, and to him who knocks, it will be opened." (Matthew 7:7 – 8) As earthly fathers give good gifts to their children, how much more will our heavenly Father give to us the Holy Spirit when we ask Him! (Luke 11:13)

Allow God to be your GPS, and you will never fail. He will guide, lead, and enable us to succeed in every effort. He will chart our course. We cannot lose. That is, we cannot lose if we allow Him to lead us. He will go to work to cause us to prosper, and He will recalibrate when we've missed the mark. He is our assurance that we will reach our destination.

Questions for Personal Reflection

Why is important to the have the Holy Spirit as the navigator in your life? (Read John14:16 – 18, 25 – 26; 1 Corinthians 12:1 – 14.)

Can you cite at least one instance in your own life in which you have seen the Holy Spirit direct your path?

Why is the Holy Spirit so critical in assisting us to make our dreams come true and in leading effectively where we are assigned?

Chapter 6

Wisdom from Above is Yours

"For the Lord gives skilful and godly Wisdom; from His mouth come knowledge and understanding." Proverbs 2:6

We have discussed the importance of overcoming our fears and being empowered by the Holy Spirit to achieve our dreams. However, without wisdom, or should I say Godly wisdom, it will be challenging to sustain our dreams or ensure success for the long term.

Wisdom is the basis for victorious living. We need the wisdom that comes from above to sustain whatever effort we are involved in. You may be knowledgeable and have the right information but, if you do not know how and when to apply it, knowledge is useless. I have seen very knowledgeable people shipwreck their lives and dreams because they have lacked wisdom. Millions of dollars have been lost on business ventures because of this.

Webster's Dictionary defines *wisdom* as insight, the ability to discern or judge what is true or right and applying the correct solution to the situation at hand. In the Message Bible,

Eugene Peterson says that *wisdom*, as used in the Bible, allows us to have an "on earth as it is in heaven everyday living experience." It is the art of living skilfully and applying the correct methods, solutions, and responses to the actual conditions in which we find ourselves. Charles H. Spurgeon says that *wisdom* is the right use of knowledge. When a man finds wisdom and gains understanding, scripture calls him blessed. That's because finding wisdom is more profitable than silver and yields a better return than gold. Nothing can compare to it (Proverbs 3:13 – 15).

Many of us have mistaken wisdom for common sense or intellectual knowledge, but those are very different than Godly wisdom. Natural wisdom comes from the world's points of view, our own experiences, or the experiences of others. While these sometimes have worth, the wisdom of the world and our experiences typically is limited and yields only short-term benefits that are conditional. However, the wisdom from God is peace-loving, full of mercy, good, impartial, and sincere (James 3:17). Godly wisdom transcends human wisdom and experience. It is available to anyone who calls on the Name of the Lord. Just think; we can go to God, the creator of the universe, who is all-knowing and who has created all things, and we can seek answers and solutions to any and every issue that concerns us. And, He shares with us freely from His own infinite wisdom. So, God grants us the highest level of understanding (Proverbs 4:7), and we are able to do what is prudent at the right time.

When we need wisdom from God, all we have to do is ask. Scripture says, "If any of you lacks wisdom, let him ask of God, who gives generously to all without finding fault, and it will be given to him." (James 1:5) When we ask God for wisdom, He does not think we are dumb. In fact, when we ask for wisdom, it is one of the ways that we demonstrate our reverence for Him and acknowledge Him as the God of wisdom, knowledge, and understanding. Also, when we ask for wisdom, it is critical that we believe that God will give us answers and spiritual insight into the issues that we face.

God expects us to come to Him first and to take His instruction and counsel (Proverbs 1:5). He is all wisdom and might. From His mouth comes knowledge and understanding (Proverbs 2:6). No other wisdom supersedes the wisdom of God (Proverbs 21:30) and, in fact, God's wisdom is able to stop the adversary in his tracks (Luke 21:15).

God will liberally give us all that we need, in particular Jesus, who has been made unto us the wisdom from God (1 Corinthians 1:30). Through Jesus, we have every answer to living a victorious life. And, at His direction, we are better equipped to lead and influence the lives of others.

Without wisdom, we spend needless time trying to figure life out on our own. However, understanding that we need the wisdom of God to do great things, and that we can accomplish little on our own, gives birth to success, favor, and happiness (Proverbs 24:13 – 14). It also brings pleasure to our Lord.

Questions for Personal Reflection

What is wisdom?

What's the source of our wisdom?

Why is wisdom so very important in living this life of faith? (Read Proverbs 3:13 – 15, James 3:17, and Isaiah 55:8 – 9.)

Chapter 7

You Have the Favor of God

"You prepare a table before me in the presence of my enemies; You anoint my head with oil; my cup runs over. Surely goodness and mercy shall follow me all the days of my life; and I will dwell in the house of the Lord forever." Psalm 23:5 – 6

F avor is God's supernatural power that affords us special privileges, preferential and unprecedented treatment, and consideration. God is the one who bestows favor and is blameless (Psalm 84:11). God's favor doesn't fade away; it lasts for a lifetime. It will cause us to stand strong and will keep us prosperous (Psalm 30:5 – 7). There is nothing that we can do to earn God's favor. It is a freely given gift of God.

One way that God gives us favor is through access to His throne, and He has done so through the finished work of Jesus Christ. Because of Christ, we now have the privilege to come boldly to His throne to receive grace (favor) and mercy in our time of need. We do not have to come crying, although He will receive our tears. Nor must we come begging, for His gift of favor is free.

As a parent desires to give his child the necessary resources to succeed in life. A parent also gives his own children rights and privileges that just are not available to other children. So it is with the Father. He loves us because we are His children; He gives us special gifts – favor and grace through His Son, the Christ. All that we need, He is able to supply. He is bountiful, and His resources are limitless. All that He has is ours. And, all of this is ours, not because of anything we have done, but it is ours because we belong to Him through Christ. Because of Christ, we are no longer guests at His table; we are partakers in His favor, kingdom of His righteousness, vessels of His Holy Spirit, and joint heirs with Christ (Romans 8:17, Ephesians 3:6). He has seated us at His banquet table, and His banner over us is love and favor.

In Christian circles, you may not hear a lot about the favor of God, but every now and then you will hear someone say that I am blessed and highly favored. You may hear this and think to yourself that the person must have an inflated sense of self-worth. But, the truth is that, as believers, we are not only to say that we are favored of God, but we are to expect it.

Our God is a God of favor and grace, and He has stacked the deck so that His children can receive all the benefits of this great salvation. It gives our Heavenly Father pleasure to give us all things we need to live a godly life. Favor is one of the benefits of our salvation and of our position as children of God. Many of us live defeated lives and lives that are below our privilege and inheritance. However, all we need to do is receive God's favor, expect it, and walk in it. Many of us are not aware of the favor upon our lives because we do not know how to recognize it when it presents itself. Yet, whether we acknowledge it or not, God's favor has been made available to everyone who has accepted Jesus as Savior and Lord. Scripture tells us that grace and truth came by Jesus Christ. Jesus became our mercy seat – the seat of grace and favor.

God's favor cannot be taken away. It lasts for a lifetime. As we see with God's promise toward Israel, favor can be generational (Isaiah 44:3). And, following Jesus, who is our model as we progress in our relationship with God, we should expect to grow in favor with God and man (Luke 2:52).

Perhaps, unlike any other, King David understood the favor of God. He knew how to ask for it and how to receive it; he expected it and knew that God would work on his behalf. When he was at war, he entreated God for favor in defeating his enemy. When in need of provision, he sought God for favor. And, when his time had come to die, he sought favor for his son, Solomon. David sought God's favor to be merciful unto him (Psalm 119:58). In Psalm 106:4, he asked God to remember him with the same sort of favor He has toward His people and to come near and rescue him. In Psalm 5:12, he reminds the Lord of the favor that he promised the right-

eous. He said "For You, Lord, will bless the [uncompromis-
ingly] righteous [him who is upright and in right standing
with you]; as with a shield you will surround him with good-
will (pleasure and favor)."

There is not a situation or circumstance that favor cannot
change. There is nothing stronger than the favor of the Lord,
and nothing can stop it or cancel it out. Any time David won
a battle, he declared that it was not by his sword or hand but
by the favor of God and His hand (Psalm 44:3).

I can clearly see how God's favor has shown up in every
aspect of my life and the life of my son. Favor presents itself
in my life every single day. Favor has opened doors that
should not have been opened to me. I've received preferential
treatment and consideration from high-profile individuals,
and I've gotten unprecedented job assignments, fellowships,
salary increases, leadership positions, and recognition. Now,
I know that none of these things came my way because of
any brilliance on my part, or because of pedigree or degrees,
but rather they were a result of God's divine favor. Like me,
my son has received abundantly in his young years because
of God's favor, favor which is generational. I've seen God's
favor turn back the hand of enemies and cause them to be
my greatest supporters. His favor has given me the fortitude
to persevere in the most unlikely and undesirable environ-
ments. I know what it is like to have God give me a party

in the midst of my enemies and to have His goodness and mercy follow me.

As God grants us favor, we must remember that the favor of God often accompanies purpose. He gives it not only for us but to bless others and to draw others to Him. He ties favor to His purposes and plans. We must keep in mind what the Psalmist said: "For God is the greatness and the power and the glory, majesty and splendour for everything in earth is His. It is His Kingdom that has been exalted and made head over all. Wealth and honor comes from Him, He is the ruler over all things and in His hands there is favor and power to exalt. He gives strength to all." (1 Chronicles 29:11 – 12)

So, embrace the generosity of God's gift to you. It is yours for the having. Recognize it, acknowledge it, receive it, expect it, thank Him for it, and then walk in it. His favor is long-standing and enduring. It is more precious than silver or gold (Proverbs 22:1). Money cannot buy it, nor can it be bartered or negotiated. Favor…its God's special gift to you.

Questions for Personal Reflection

What is favor?

Why is favor important in a believer's life?

What kind of favor do you need today? (Read Psalm 5:12 and Psalm 23.)

Chapter 8

Prayer a Gift and a Weapon from God

And pray in the Spirit on all occasions with all kinds of prayers and requests. With this in mind, be alert and always keep on praying for all the Lord's people (Ephesians 6: 18)

Prayer is one of the greatest gifts to us from our Father. He gives us the extraordinary privilege and opportunity to meet with Him at any time to discuss anything anywhere. Prayer is one of our most vital practices and at the core of our personal relationship with God. It is one of the ways that we communicate with our Heavenly Father. In our conversations, we hear His voice; our desires are declared; and our hope is restored. Forgiveness is given; grace is imparted; dependence on God is realized; and our trust and faith in Him is strengthened. It is a time of fellowship, friendship, and intimacy with our Lord. It is about talking *and* listening. It is about knowing that God is aware of everything that we are experiencing and that He is present to hear and respond.

As many think, prayer isn't about our posture – the way we sit, stand, or kneel. It isn't about our location; prayer can happen anywhere – in a car, lying on the bed, walking the streets. God is everywhere, and His Spirit lives in us.

Prayer isn't about grammar or a particular way the words should be enunciated. It can be as simple as a whispered "Help me Lord," or it can follow the pattern that was given us in the Lord's Prayer (Matthew 6:9-13). In fact, we do not have to depend on ourselves for the words at all; the Holy Spirit, who abides in us, gives us the right words to pray. He comes alongside us, helping us to say what it is in our hearts. If we do not know how to pray or what to pray in certain circumstances, it doesn't matter. He will do the praying for us and through us with wordless signs and aching groans. He knows us far better than we know ourselves. He knows our condition and keeps us present before God. That's why we can be sure that every detail in our lives God works together for our good (Roman 8:26-28).

Our Father desires us to come to Him and share our thoughts and hearts. He waits patiently to hear our voices. God wants to help us and he can through prayer. Psalm 50:15 says that when we call on God in our day of trouble, he rescues and delivers us. You have not done, and never will do, anything that makes you worthy of this generous gift. It is given just because God loves you and wants to be in fellowship with you. Communicating with God has residual benefits; prayers are answered and we are refreshed, restored and satisfied.

You do not have to be a gifted orator to pray, nor do you have to be an adult to pray. This gift is given to His children, regardless of race or ethnicity, age, gender, or status in the community or the church. If anyone has accepted Christ as Savior, God hears his prayers. And, for anyone who has not chosen to follow Christ, God promises to hear a sinner's repentant prayer and to welcome you from death into life, from exclusion to inclusion in the family of faith. When we receive and accept this gift of prayer, we can enter into the glorious presence of our Father. Prayer should be as natural as drinking and eating.

Prayer can also be used as a weapon against the attacks of the enemy. We can directly speak to God and he will give us specific strategies to stop, hinder an abort the enemy's attacks. Prayer is so powerful that it can change the course of a nation or its events. When God wants to change things and events, he uses our voices to communicate his desires orally to him and among others. When Solomon's time had come to be the King over Israel, God said, that if his people who are called by my name, would humble themselves and pray and seek his face and turn from their wicked ways, then he would hear them, forgive their sin and will heal their land (2 Chronicles 7:14).

Prayer can heal our country, heal our marriages, impact the outcomes of wars, break the shackles of bondage, give divine direction and strategies, affect generations to come and pro-duce wonderful results. Scripture also informs us that "when our prayers are offered in faith, the sick person will be made well, and the Lord will raise him up. If they have sinned, they will be forgiven. Therefore confess your sins to each other and pray for each other so that you may be healed. The prayer of a righteous person is powerful and effective (James 5: 15-16)."

When we pray, we can be assured of one thing and that our God hears and answers our prayers (John 14:14).

Questions for Personal Reflection

What is prayer?

Why is prayer important?

Do you pray? If so, how often and for what?

What is the Lord's Prayer? Is it a model to be followed or a prayer that we should pray? (Matthew 6:9-13 & 1 Thessalonians 5:17)

Chapter 9

Fulfilling God's Call in the Marketplace

"God is marshalling his people in the workplace as never before in history. God is up to something. The next spiritual awakening could take place in the marketplace." Henry Blackaby

What is the marketplace, and why is it important? The marketplace is where people live, thrive, and make a living. It is a defined in the Greek as a place of public assembly. It is the place where people meet, do business, exchange information, and find community.

We read in the Bible that Jesus Christ was often in the marketplace, not to sell anything, but meeting with people and preaching the Gospel of the Kingdom of God. In fact, the marketplace was where Jesus did most of His ministry. It's where we see Him healing the sick, raising the dead, and speaking about the wonders of God.

Jesus' disciples were tapped from the marketplace. Peter was a fisherman; Matthew was a tax collector; and Luke was a physician. The marketplace also was the center of ministry in the early church. It was where people worked and where they met to buy their goods and sell their wares. Many men and women in the Bible were in full-time ministry and worked full-time in business. God used marketplace ministry to connect His will and His kingdom purpose to the vocations, gifting, passions, and life purposes of His servants. By partnering with God in this way, they each became His ambassadors in the marketplace.

Today's women also are in the marketplace...sometimes we are there more than we are in our homes. However, we shouldn't view that time in the marketplace as unrelated to ministry. As fellow workers with Christ, we have the privilege of serving God through the work that we do -- no matter where it is and no matter when we do it. Everything that we have belongs to God and has been given for His purpose. All gifts, talents, abilities, and knowledge are to be used wherever God assigns us, and it is kingdom work – even when the assignment is outside the conventional boundaries of the church.

The reality is that ministry is not reserved just for ministers in the church. We all have been called and invited by God to be ministers of reconciliation in the marketplace – wherever that is for us. We are not to fragment the exercise of our faith and reserve it only for church. Instead, we are to use our God-given gifts everywhere we go – using them for God and His purposes.

Just as He did with women, like Dorcas and Lydia, in the Bible, God is still raising up women today in the marketplace to be salt and light in the world. Women are discovering their passions and giftedness, and are creating opportunities for employment, supplementing their families' income, and doing ministry. As women of faith, we are being uniquely positioned to be an influence, not only in the home but in the marketplace as well. We have been called to bring the Kingdom of God to the marketplace, to be extensions of His grace to many who will come to know the Lord through us.

Many Christians cannot grasp that God can use us in the marketplace to glorify Him as well as the church. However, in some respects, the marketplace is just the place where God desires us most to do His work. And, scripture supports this. Think about The Great Commission. Jesus commanded to His followers to *"Go into the entire world…"* to share the Good News (Matthew 28:18 – 20). If we are to achieve this great commission, we have to move beyond the walls of the church; consequently, we've got work to do – kingdom work – in the marketplace to follow Christ's command to touch the lives of the lost. Don't misunderstand. I am not minimizing or devaluing the absolutely vital work that happens in church. However, there is a world outside of the local church – in the marketplace – just waiting to be won for Christ. We have been called to be *in* the world (though not *of* the world), living out our faith and introducing others to the saving grace of Christ.

Faith is not to be practiced only inside the walls of the church. For the Christian, faith is life. Faith goes everywhere you go, including to work. If you're living and growing in Christ, it's impossible to compartmentalize your faith and reserve it for church. Instead, you begin to recognize that you live to do the will of God and to express who He is and what He has done anywhere you are. You do so to honor God, and you do so to share His grace to a world in need of a Savior. You see, there really is no separation between your vocation and your faith. The marketplace simply becomes your mission field; it's where lives can be led from darkness to the light.

Questions for Personal Reflection

What is marketplace ministry?

Was Jesus a marketplace minister? Why or why not?

Why is it essential to lead where you are? (Read Matthew 20:1 – 7, 28:18 – 20, and John 17.)

Chapter 10

Healing and Impacting Your World for God

"You are a chosen race, a royal priesthood, a holy nation, God's own people, in order that you may proclaim the mighty acts of Him who called you out of darkness, into His marvelous light." 1 Peter 2:9

W omen are, and have been, vital contributors to resolving community problems. Women bring new perspectives and valuable insight to community issues. We often are naturals at building relationship and helping others, which can be critical to making things better. And, women are skilled at empowering people to achieve their dreams and potential.

The modern Christian woman follows a lineage of strong and courageous women who have given their lives for the needs of others. Consider Mother Theresa, who gave her life to care for millions who lacked basic human resources. Take Harriet Tubman, the abolitionist, who sought freedom for the slaves by helping them escape through the Underground Railroad. These, and countless others, played significant roles in their communities and were used to impact generations. These women were God's change agents.

As today's Christian women, we are being called to do the same. You don't have to be Mother Theresa or Harriet Tubman to be used in the community to effect positive change for humanity's good. Unlike in some arenas, community leadership often poses fewer obstacles for women to become involved and play leadership roles. With the Holy Spirit's empowerment and guidance, Christian women can reach beyond their homes and work and find themselves actively engaged in community, solving problems and improving the lives of families. Their life experiences from home and work qualify them to do an excellent job as community leaders.

Becoming an effective community leader is a process. It may begin with becoming a part of a small group that is focused on a community issue, such as adolescent drug use, or by accepting a volunteer position with the local PTA. Starting small isn't bad. These small beginnings will help you identify your leadership capabilities and particular leadership style. Small starts also may help you develop networking skills. By engaging in community work, you also will have the opportunity to bring the Christian influence and perspective into addressing community problems and issues.

If you want to begin this journey of community involvement, here are a few steps that you may want to consider to get started:

1. Determine the group or project in which you want to become involved. Consider volunteering initially to learn about the group, issues, and the project.
2. Increase your knowledge. Learn as much as you can about the problems facing your community. Research possible solutions to the problems. Ask God for wisdom about when to speak and how to add to the conversation.
3. Take on responsibility. Volunteer to do extra work and to support the leader.
4. Invest time in the project. As opportunities arise, offer to help, and be willing to take on leadership roles.
5. Focus on your successes more than your failures. Do what you can to learn from your failures, but don't dwell on them.

People will begin to recognize your leadership abilities and give you more responsibility. Before you know it, you may be the next community leader.

Questions for Personal Reflection

Have you been called to lead in your community?

If community leadership is for you, what are some of the steps you have taken so far to achieve your dream? What more can you do?

If you don't feel that you're being called to lead, is there something else you can do to be an influence for Christ in your community?

Explain why Jesus was a community man? (Read Luke 2:41 – 49.)

Chapter 11

Called to Politics

"Let every person be subject to the governing authorities. For there is no authority except from God, and those that exist have been instituted by God. Therefore whoever resists the authorities resists what God has appointed, and those who resist will incur judgment." Romans 13:1 – 2

S hould a Christian woman become involved in, or strive for a leadership role in, politics? The answer is "yes," if that is what God is calling her to do.

The Christian voice in politics is necessary if we are to inform public policy and laws with a Christian world view. As women leaders, we cannot afford to sit on the sidelines and not become involved. The time has come for women to be agents of change, political compasses, taking an active role in the decision making concerning our families, our health, and our communities.

It is nothing new for Christian women to be involved in politics. The difference today may be that, with so many modes of communication, more people are aware of what is happening beyond their own communities. Yet, there are countless women who have contributed to our society politically. For example, Frances Willard led the temperance (anti-alcohol) movement in the 19th century. Women were in the forefront of the abolitionist and Civil Rights movements – women, such as Sojourner Truth, Harriet Tubman, Frances Ellen Watkins Harper, Maria W. Stewart, and Rosa Parks. Others played significant roles in the effort to have the Equal Rights Amendment passed in the 1970s. In more recent years, there are examples, like Beverly La Haye, who mobilized hundreds of thousands of American women to support the pro-life movement and the notion of traditional marriage.

Today, we have Christian women as mayors; city, county, state, and federal legislators; governors; other government officials; and even Supreme Court justices. These women are informing policy, developing legislation, and impacting the way that government operates on a daily basis. They have become a voice for those who may not have a voice.

Although we've focused on "modern-day" politically active women, this is not a new phenomenon. The Bible points to some of our greatest women leaders. In the Bible, we find examples, such as Deborah and Huldah. Deborah became a judge at a time when Israel was experiencing a spiritual and moral decline, partly due to the loss of their national leaders, Moses and Joshua (Judges 4 & 5). Huldah was a prophetess, on whom the king relied to interpret the law (2 Kings 22:14 – 20). These were women with political influence.

God desires His presence to be exhibited everywhere, and He often chooses to do so through us. Our godly influence can do the world good. We can make important contributions to addressing the needs of our world – not based on what we think we should do but exercising the wisdom of God.

The church has a responsibility to ensure that there is a righteous voice in politics. Consider it an excellent profession in which to model Jesus' leadership style. Consider the number of lives that can be touched through this type of ministry. Consider the good that can be done, as you advocate for the concerns and issues that are real, and often unmet, in the lives of so many.

Could God be calling you to be His voice in a particular political sphere? If you feel that He is calling you, here are few strategies that may help get you started:

1. Honestly assess your current situation. What are your family and job responsibilities? If you are married, does your spouse support this desire? How will you balance your responsibilities at home and/or at work with your pursuit to become more politically active?

2. Begin by taking baby steps into the political process. Start by becoming involved in your local PTA, women's auxiliary, or another community group. Just get started! Then,

look for opportunities to get your feet wet in leadership positions.

3. If it appears that politics is right for you, look for mentors in government or politics at the local, county, or state level. Other options might be to locate a political mentoring program or volunteer to be a part of a think tank on a community issues.

4. Visit your legislators, and see if they will allow you to shadow them.

5. Volunteer for an unpaid internship several days a week in an area that interests you, or volunteer to work on a campaign in the area where you live.

6. Join a political group.

7. Attend political rallies.

8. Look for training opportunities that offer you the opportunity to learn about community issues.

9. Build connections across race and class. This encourages and reinforces a sense of mutual respect, responsibility, relationship.

10. Become known in your community for producing good work.

11. Finally, do not forget your faith, values, and morals. You are God's ambassador in this setting; represent Him well.

Questions for Personal Reflection

Do you vote in each election? Why, or why not?

Why is the Christian's voice needed in politics?

Take some time in scripture to identify some of the Old Testament and New Testament leaders involved in politics. Are there traits that you see in them that you also see in yourself?

Chapter 12

Reflecting Christ in Your Homes

"The wise woman builds her house, but with her own hands the foolish one tears hers down." Proverbs 14:1

W hether society acknowledges motherhood as a leadership job or not, it is. Leadership responsibilities, for many women, rest solidly in the home.

I was reading an article recently about living holy lives. The thing that resonated with me most was what the author said about our homes. He likened our homes to being small churches, filled with God and the richness of our faith. In other words, first and foremost, our homes should reflect our faith, and our actions there should demonstrate the indwelt Christ and His character. Unfortunately, this is not always the case for many of us. We are totally different people in our homes than we are at church.

Whether you are single, married, or divorced; whether you are living with your spouse, children, other family members, or alone, one point is always true. *How* we live affects those *with whom* we live.

As Jesus' lights in the world, we also should be His lights in our homes. Scripture informs us that, as women (particularly those of us who are older), we are to be reverent in behavior, not given to malicious gossip, not drinking much wine, encouraging younger women to love their husbands and children, sensible workers at home, kind, and (if we are married) subject to our own husbands. What's the reason for such behavior? It's so that the word of God may not be dishonored in the world (Titus 2:3 – 5).

Our righteous living has the ability to affect our spouses for good. In the Garden of Eden, God brought Eve to Adam in order to give him a helper suitable for him (Genesis 2:18 – 25). And so, as Christian women partner with their husbands to make a home, raise a family, minister together in whatever calling God has given to them as a couple, they have the ability to fulfil God's specially chosen mission in their lives.

Some Christian women, though, are joined to unbelieving husbands or those who are not strong in the faith. Marriage is challenging enough, but couple that challenge with having an unbelieving spouse or one who's struggling with his faith, and the challenge is compounded. That is one reason why the Bible warns against being unequally yoked together with unbelievers (2 Corinthians 6:14). In marriage, you are supposed to be working in tandem with another person, moving in the same direction, at the same speed, for the same reasons.

The strain, stemming from your faith differences, has the ability to impact the marital relationship and engender disharmony in the home.

Yet, the Bible provides hope, even in these situations. In 1 Peter 3:1 – 2, women are instructed to make their lifestyles such that, even an unbelieving husband may be won to Christ because of how she conducts herself. Although it is tempting, the woman's role is not to try to coerce change. (That usually backfires.) Her role is to be obedient to God's instruction. Only God can change a life. However, He often uses us as instruments of His grace, to show forth kindness, love, and tenderness – all attributes that God first showed to us – and in so doing (and with much prayer), do our part in introducing that spouse to the Christ that we know and love.

Sharing one's faith does not end with a spouse. As mothers, we should be the first to share our faith with our children. Living out our faith is a necessity, for our efforts at righteous living serve as a model of how godly lives should be lived. Often, the mother is the one shaping a child during the formative years and ensuring that the child has the most appropriate conditions in which to grow and reach his or her highest potential.

Mothers always have had a strong influence on their children. The Bible portrays for us the constant presence of Mary in the life of Jesus. Another example is Hannah, the mother of Samuel, who, even after waiting so long for his birth, dedi-cated her son to the work of God. As a result, Samuel became a priest, prophet, and the final judge of Israel. (1 Samuel 1, 2, and 7) It is no different today. Many of current leaders credit their mothers as being instrumental in their success.

One thing that mothers must remember is that our behav-iour is being observed daily, and often is mirrored, by our children. It is important that we demonstrate Christ in our lives by showing love, grace, and kindness. Believe it or not, when we live righteously, we encourage others to do the same. In our homes, we have the opportunity, and the responsibility, to establish a standard for holy living. Scrip-ture instructs us to keep the commandments of God our-selves and to teach our children (in a variety of ways) to rev-erence Him so that they will have a peaceful and fruitful life (Deuteronomy 6:1 – 9).

If we let the light of God flow through us, we would be amazed at the wonderful work that God is just waiting to do in the lives of our family members. Before you know it, things in your home will change for the good. The spouse, who may have had difficulty with his faith, may just wake up one morning, offer to join you at church, and accept Christ. Your children may rise up and call you blessed (Proverbs 31:28), as they see you loving right before them.

There are blessings for the woman who endeavours to live a righteous life. She is a delight to Lord and a sweet fragrance to her household.

Questions for Personal Reflection

What types of influence could a woman have on her family?

Read Proverbs 31:10 – 31. What are some of the praise-worthy attributes found in this passage?

Be honest. How would your family describe you today?

What could you begin doing differently now to improve the environment of your home?

Chapter 13

Using Your Gifts in the Church

As each has received a gift, use it to serve one another, as good stewards of God's varied grace: whoever speaks, as one who speaks oracles of God; whoever serves, as one who serves by the strength that God supplies — in order that in everything God may be glorified through Jesus Christ. To him belong glory and dominion forever and ever 1 Peter 4:10-11.

A s women of faith we called to practice our gifts in the local assembly or church. You may have opted not to become a member of a local church. But, I ask you, is that living out your faith? You may come to church every Sunday. But, is church attendance alone exercising your faith? I think not. You may feel that, because you're not a preacher, teacher, usher, or choir member, you have nothing to contribute in your local assembly. Quite the contrary, God has given each of us gifts, and all parts of this body called "church" are called to use what we've been given.

The church has a mandate from God to preach the gospel, develop believers, and meet their spiritual and physical needs. No, you may not have a title or receive a church salary, but you have gifts, talents, abilities, and knowledge that God has given you to edify, strengthen, encourage, nurture, counsel, inspire, and care for those in the local church and, through the church, in your community. God is depending on each of us to help bring others into His kingdom and, once there, to bring the body into spiritual maturity.

How has God equipped us to serve the body? Some have been prepared to serve in official roles – as apostles, evangelists, pastors, and teachers – to edify the body of Christ (Ephesians 4:11, 12). Others, God has given the word of wisdom – the ability to share wise advice, from God's perspective. Some receive the gift of knowledge – to provide supernatural understanding and special insight into situations. Some are gifted with great faith, special healing, miracles, prophesy, administration, hospitality, the ability to speak in unknown languages, or discernment.

All of these gifts come from the Spirit of God. He alones determines the gift(s) a person should have (1 Corinthians 12). And, He alone directs us how to best use our gifts to serve in the body. Although our gifts may be different, they all come from the same source, the Spirit of God. He is the One who works through every gift and is in us all.

Every gift is designed to help the body grow spiritually and to be strengthened so that it, in turn, will function according to God's purpose.

Have you identified the ways that God has gifted you? What are the spiritual gifts He has entrusted to you? What are the other skills and abilities you have that could be used for the kingdom? Why not take some time with God and reflect on not only how He has blessed you but also how He wants those gifts, skills, and abilities to be used.

Every person has a function in the body and a role to play. No, you may not sing like an angel, but you sure can bake a cake, or clean a house, or drive a truck. No, you may not teach or preach, but you can edit sermons or build pews. Whatever God has placed in your hand is useful for kingdom purposes. And, that's just the way He intended it.

Questions for Personal Reflection:

What gifts, skills, and abilities has God placed in you?

Are you using your gifts and abilities to edify and aid the spiritual growth of the church? If so, how? If not, why not?

Chapter 14

Abiding in the Vine-Your Key to Success

"I am the vine, you are the branches. He who abides in Me, and I in him, bears much fruit; for without Me you can do nothing." John 15:5

I n this fast moving world, a long-term *anything* is rare. People are constantly looking for something new or an updated version of what they already have. We're continually seeking the next adventure, connection, job, or relationship. Very few of us stick with anything for very long.

For many of us, this even applies to Christ. We accept Christ as Savior, and that's good. But, then, as soon as the honeymoon is over, we're looking for what's next. However, this faith walk isn't about pit stops and continual upgrades. If we are to grow strong in our Christian faith, impact the world for Christ, and fulfil our God-given dreams, we must learn something about *abiding*.

Scripture tells us that we can't bear fruit – that is, we can't accomplish anything useful – unless we abide in Him (John

15:1 – 8). Only by abiding in Christ can we reach our full potential and do the work that we've been called to do.

Abiding means staying connected to, and learning from, Christ. We come to appreciate that He is the source from which we draw our strength, power, direction, love, and abundant life. Only in His presence can we find His heart and will for our lives.

How does one stay connected – *abide* – in Christ on a continual basis? Doing so actually is very achievable. We do not have to go to a special location to be in communion with Christ, because *we* are the temple of Holy Spirit; the Spirit of Christ dwells in us. His abiding presence already has taken up residence in each believer (1 Corinthians 3:16) and waits to be acknowledged by us.

So, you acknowledge Christ's presence in you, and join Him in an abiding relationship, in any number of ways. As we worship and praise Him, we're abiding with Him, for He makes His presence known by inhabiting the praises of His people (Psalm 22:3). As we study the Word, He will reveal Himself to us, and His words will come alive, renewing our minds and generating new life within us according to His will and design. As we speak His Word, we see His Spirit go to work to implement His will. As we minister to others, we see the fruit of His presence blossoming. As we spend time in

God's presence, we find that He shows us the path of life and reveals to us joy and eternal pleasures (Psalm 16:11).

We were created for fellowship and communion with God. Only by remaining in His presence can we come know joy, satisfaction, and the fulfillment of the dreams He has given to us. In His presence, we can be at peace that, where He assigns us, His presence will empower us to go. In His presence, we know that, following His plan pleases and glorifies Him.

So if you are abiding in Christ's presence, woman of faith, feel free to dream. You have the guarantee that, if you continue to remain in Christ, every dream will come true.

Questions for Personal Reflection

What does abiding in Christ mean to you?

Why does abiding in Christ help you bear more and more fruit?

What are you doing now to remain in fellowship with Christ?

What could you do differently to abide even more?

It's Your Time

It's your time to rise and take your place

It's time to conquer fear

And to take hold of faith

It's time to embrace the Holy Spirit

And receive his guidance and love

It's time to ask for wisdom from above

It's time to pray as never before

It is time to recognize what a special treasure

you are to God

It's time to dream big and watch God open doors

It's time to walk in his favor and embrace his call

It' time to rise and lead others to his immeasurable

and incomprehensible grace

It's time to move forward and take your place.

References

1. G.L. "Labor of Women in the Gospel", Trumpet 95
2. Doherty, W.J., "Take Back Your Marriage", 2001
3. "Equipping Women of Faith for Success in Business", National Association of Christian Women in Business, 2010; http. www.nacwb.org
4. Crittenden, Ann, "The Price of Motherhood", 2001
5. Dash, R, 11 Principles of entrepreneurial leadership
6. Woolf, Jamie, "Mom and Chief: How Wisdom from the Workplace Can Save Your Family from Chaos", www.momsinchief.com
7. Jaynes, Sharon, "Dreams of Every Woman: And How God Wants to Fulfil Them"
8. Empowering Christian women.com
9. "Worship that Brings Down the Presence of God": Practicing the Presence of God. Soaking in his Presence, www.secretplaceministries.org;
10. Kehler, "Katherine J, " Dreaming God's Dream, www.powertochange.org
11. Message Bible
12. Amplified Bible
13. NIV Bible
14. The New Living Bible
15. Meyers, Joyce, Battlefield of the Mind, 1982

CPSIA information can be obtained at www.ICGtesting.com
Printed in the USA
BVOW081927200812

298370BV00001B/48/P